A #ashtag A Day

——◄ ⫷⫸ ►——

30 DAY DEVOTIONAL WITH

Vikkie J

A #ashtag A Day

---◁‖▷---

30 DAY DEVOTIONAL WITH

Vikkie J

Contents

Introduction 7

Acknowledgements 9

Day 1: *#peace* 11

Day 2: *#praycontinually* 13

Day 3: *#liveyourbestlife* 15

Day 4: *#smile* 17

Day 5: *#believe* 19

Day 6: *#mercy* 21

Day 7: *#heartposture* 23

Day 8: *#becontent* 25

Day 9: *#praise* 27

Day 10: *#unbothered* 29

Day 11: *#trust* 31

Day 12: *#conversewithGod* 33

Day 13: *#submit* 35

Day 14: *#selfworth* 37

Day 15: *#renewyourmind* 39

Day 16: *#friendships* 41

Day 17: *#visions* 43

Day 18: *#desires* 45

Day 19: *#bekind* 47

Day 20: *#faith* 49

Day 21: *#saved* 51

Day 22: *#love* 53

Day 23: *#noweapon* 55

Day 24: *#overcomer* 57

Day 25: *#temple* 59

Day 26: *#testify* 61

Day 27: *#purpose* 63

Day 28: *#workingforGod* 65

Day 29: *#Embraceyou* 67

Day 30: *#bepatient* 69

Day 31: *#beyou* 71

Conclusion 73

Introduction

I wrote this devotional to encourage you. I believe my purpose in life is simple, to encourage you. Life has so much to offer sometimes, it's joy, peace, & prosperity, and other times it brings discouragement, sorrow, & pain. No matter what life brings, just remember God has the final say. Each daily devotional ends with a hashtag. Why? Great question! Life is super busy for everyone. For many of us, we desire to spend more time with God and meditate on His word. But with all the other entities vying for our attention, sometimes God and His word gets pushed down to the bottom of our "to-do list." So I thought, if I wrote a short daily devotional focusing on 1 concept, and attach a hashtag to it, then it might help others focus on God throughout their day. I just know God has a special plan for your life, so let us tackle the next 30 days together with the full expectation that you'll experience the promises of God in order to live your best life while standing on the foundation of God's living word.

Acknowledgements

I wrote this devotional mostly in secret. I have to thank God for placing the desire in my heart. Because of Him, I had the courage to pick up the pin & write. Those who know me well know that I'm not the best writer, I can butcher a word via text, and God knows I often mispronounce words, however somehow God saw fit to entrust me with writing this devotional for you.

As I desire to encourage & cheer for others to live their best life for Christ, I'm so grateful for my personal cheerleader, my husband, Trevor. You believe in me when I don't believe in myself. You speak life over me when life seems to knock me down. God truly gave me His very best when he gave me you.

When I started this devotional, we hadn't started our family. To our Bella, your presence enhances my desire to reflect God's character. Your presence enhances my desire to operate in the fruits of the holy spirit daily so that I'm presenting the best version of myself. For parents are children's first representation of Christ. Bella, you are our special blessing from God.

Lastly, I'd like to thank my friends who knew of this secret desire to write this devotional & provided unlimited support & accountability. Thank you, Kristina, Altimese, Nikolai, Abigail, Tiona, & Tia E. Thank you Shayla for being obedient, operating in your gift, & confirming what God told me in August 2022 which was "Finish the book."

Day 1

Peace I leave with you, my peace I give you. I do not give to you as the world gives. Do not let your hearts be troubled and do not be afraid.

John 14:27 NIV

We were never promised that life wouldn't bring us fear, anger, hurt, or disappointment. Or that every day would be filled with happiness, success, & joy. But how comforting it is to know that God freely provides His peace during every season of our lives. I've struggled for years to truly receive God's peace. I'd read this scripture, proclaim it, but was unable to allow myself to receive His peace. One day in desperate need of His peace, I had to go a little further than just reading I had to pray "Lord help me receive your peace." Then I proclaimed, "I receive your peace." Often in life when someone gives us something, there may be "strings attached." The giver may expect something in return. In this scripture God is giving us his peace, no strings attached. No "I owe you." Can I encourage you today? Grab, receive, & proclaim the free peace that God is offering you....it's waiting on you.

#peace

Day 2

Pray continually

1 Thessalonians 5:17 NIV

Webster defines prayer as "to address God or a god with adoration, confession, supplication, or thanksgiving." Let's be honest, we're looking at this scripture and the first thought that comes to mind is " really, how can I do that, life is busy." I agree. You may also be thinking continually means without stopping or interrupting. I agree. I believe the Apostle Paul was speaking about a lifestyle. When we think about a lifestyle of prayer, it suddenly makes the word "continually" seems achievable. And if we dissect the definition provided we'll see that prayer can really be conversational. Remember, a conversation is a two-way street. So yes, we can pray while washing dishes, at the grocery store, or at work, but remember that sometimes we have to set aside special times so we can also hear God without interruptions.

#**praycontinually**

Day 3

The thief comes only to steal, kill, & destroy, I have come that you may have life, & have it to the full.

John 10:10 NIV

We all want to live our best life. Right? In today's society & age of social media "your best life" may mean name-brand clothing, 6 figure or greater salary, a big house & fancy car. But an abundant Godly life isn't or doesn't start or stop at the material things. I believe that God cares about every area of our lives which includes our spirituality, our finances, our relationships, our mental health, & our physical health. When the thief comes to steal, kill, & destroy he often does so when access to one, a few, or all of these 5 areas are gained. What does an abundant life look like to you in each of those 5 areas listed above?

#liveyourbestlife

Day 4

A happy heart makes the face cheerful but heartache crushes the spirit.

Proverbs 15:13 NIV

Did you know it takes more facial muscles to frown than to smile? Well, that's what they told us in physical therapy school in anatomy. Yes, life can offer all kinds of emotions that leave you wanting to do everything BUT smile. Remember, our God has been good to us. When you think of His love, mercy, & blessings how could you NOT smile? Sometimes you may feel like you have no reason to smile, and your circumstances my totally validate your feelings. Can I encourage you today, to find one reason to smile? Did you get your reason? Now ask your self "why" does that make me smile?

Here's where I get "life coachy" on you, ready? Focus on your "why" throughout the day to allow your heart to be happy. Then at the end of the day, reflect upon how many times you smiled & how you felt.

#smile

Day 5

Immediately the boy's father exclaimed, "I do believe; help me overcome my unbelief."

Mark 9:24 NIV

The boy referred to in the above verse was described as being possessed by a deaf & mute spirit. The spirit would cause the boy to foam at the mouth, gnash his teeth, & become rigid. The father shares with Jesus that the spirit has often thrown the boy into the fire & water in attempts to kill him.

The father's response above came after Jesus said *"Everything is possible for one who believes."*

My question for you today is, "what have you been believing God for, yet you have some unbelief?" How can both belief and unbelief dwell together and there be a favorable outcome?

Let's dedicate being consistent in believing what God says. What has God said personally to you? We must continue to believe in God in order for everything He has said or promised to be possible in our lives. I'm not just saying this to sound "good." In 2006 it was prophesied to me that God was "lining up my husband." At the time I was in undergrad school & dating a guy who was toxic to my mental health. I believed God but didn't know who, when, or how we would meet. Well, I met my husband in grad school 4 years later. We married 3 years later. I chose to believe God over a 7 year period. Will you?

#**believe**

Day 6

Blessed are the merciful, for they shall receive mercy.

Matthew 5:7 NIV

We've all needed a little mercy at some point in our lives. *Mercy* is compassion or forgiveness shown toward someone whom it is within one's power to punish or harm. The Bible tells us that we're blessed when we are merciful. I have yet to meet a person who doesn't want to be blessed. How often do you show mercy? Can I be honest, I have a strong disdain for calling a service provider only to get a recording for the first 3 minutes I'm on the phone. By the time I finally speak to a human, after hitting "0" or saying "representative" 20x the word mercy is often not in my vocabulary. Or how about the new cashier learning how to operate her register thus her line is super long and you've had a long day and still have to cook dinner once you get home. Compassion is free. And the world is watching God's children. Trust me, someone is ALWAYS watching you. Let's commit to showing mercy as a part of our character. Remember you'll be blessed.

#**mercy**

Day 7

But the Lord said to Samuel, "Do not consider his appearance or his height, for I have rejected him. The Lord does not look at the things people look at. People look at the outward appearance, but the Lord looks at the heart."

1 Samuel 16:7 NIV

Recently my husband & I were reflecting on our year 6 of marriage. We branded it "the year of transition" but honestly God revealed this during my quiet time with him. What we realized as we remembered all God had done for us, before the answered prayer, dream, or prophesy came to pass God tested our heart posture. Many times we witnessed others around us receive the very things we had prayed for, dreamed of, or had prophesied. We came to the conclusion that in every instance when it was our season to receive from God it was definitely the right timing, but we were also positioned not just in the physical realm but spiritually as well so that God got all the glory. God is always looking at our hearts, while a man will look at outward appearances.

#**heartposture**

Day 8

I know what it is to be in need, and I know what it is to have plenty. I have learned the secret of being content in any and every situation, whether well fed or hungry, whether living in plenty or in want.

Philippians 4:12 NIV

I'll be the first to say, that operating in contentment in whatever situation can be challenging. Contentment definitely has to be a choice. We live in a world that tells us more is better, more is greater, and more is what we should strive for. Let's seek our Father in Heaven to share the secret of contentment in our lives as He did with Paul.

#becontent

Day 9

"*I tell you, he replied, "if they keep quiet, the stones will cry out.*"

Luke 19:40 NIV

Jesus was responding to the Pharisees because they wanted Jesus to rebuke his disciples. Our God is so dope that because of who he is, even if we don't praise him he will still get his due praise.

What has God done for you today that warrants offering up praises to him? I know surely you won't let a rock out do your praise.

#**praise**

Day 10

You keep in perfect peace those whose minds are steadfast because they trust in you.

Isaiah 26:3 NIV

Have you ever known someone who's a believer that went through a difficult time? They may have had every reason to be angry with their situation & everyone involved yet this person had an undeniable unexplainable peace. I call this being unbothered. When we keep God in the forefront of all we do he will keep us in perfect peace. A peace so perfect it may not make sense to those around you. Sometimes it may not make sense to you but because you trust in God you don't see what's in the natural realm. You don't become discouraged because you keep your eyes on the things of the spiritual realm. So, let's choose today to allow God to keep us in his perfect peace.

#unbothered

Day 11

Trust in the Lord with all your heart & lean not on your own understanding.

Proverbs 3:5 NIV

Trust is defined as a firm belief in the reliability, truth, ability, or strength of someone or something. Do you really trust God with all your heart? Is God & His will the only plan for your life or is there a plan B? When I sat for the physical therapy board 4x before passing, my trust in God was tested. It took me 2 years before I became a licensed physical therapist. Throughout those 2 years, I had many nights where I cried. Countless thoughts of how it didn't seem fair. I didn't understand at first why I had to take the exam so many times before passing. I didn't understand why God wouldn't allow for my efforts, the long nights of studying, the drives to another city for tutoring not to pay off. When I finally decided to give up, to give it all to God, and trust his plan, his timing, not leaning on my own plan & timing, that's when I passed. I had to get to the point where I fully trusted God's plan, even if that meant not ever passing the test.

#**trust**

Day 12

The Lord is near to all who call on him, to all who call on him in truth.

Psalm 145: 18 NIV

Do you converse with God? God wants to be involved with you & every aspect of your life. Just like you call or text your best friend, God desires for you to talk to Him. And friend, please know that how you talk to God may look different than how I talk to God, and that's ok! Our God is all about relationships. Think about it, how do you grow more intimate with a spouse or a close friend? I'm not talking about physical intimacy. You do so by spending time with each other and having meaningful interactions and conversations.

#conversewithGod

Day 13

Submit yourselves, then to God. Resist the devil, and he will flee from you.

James 4:7 NIV

Submit is defined as accepting or yielding to a superior force or to the authority or will of another person. I know most of us, including myself, can get "caught-up" in our feelings when we hear the word submit. But the truth is we do it every single day by following protocol at work, stopping at a red light, or filing our taxes. And don't each of these things listed benefit us in some way or form? How much more of a benefit it is for us when we submit to God, His commands, and His will for our life?

#submit

Day 14

*I praise you because I am fearfully and won-
derfully made; your works are wonderful I
know that full well.*

Psalm 138:14 NIV

What's your sense of self-value or self-worth? Is
it attached to a title, a person, or a salary? Can
I make a personal confession? For years I have
measured my self-worth based on the titles in
front and at the back of my name. My husband
would tell me all the time, my worth isn't measured by titles. However, after becoming a mom
who stays at home, I was forced to re-evaluate
my self-value, how much or little I value myself
and my worth. This scripture in Psalm states
that God's works are wonderful. Then the au-
thor ends by saying "I know that full well." Do

you, my friend know how wonderful you are?
Do you know your self-worth?

#selfworth

Day 15

Do not conform to the pattern of this world but be transformed by the renewing of your mind.

Romans 12:2

There's a reason why the world has so many books centered around your thoughts, your mind, your mentality. Everything starts & ends with our thoughts. The devil knows this, that's why it's so important to get your mind right, allowing the word of God and His holy spirit to renew you daily. Have you ever had a goal? What happened in order for that goal to become a goal? You thought about it first, right, because before you could transform the goal into reality it had to be a thought. There's a quote that says you become what you think about. This is why it's imperative that we renew our minds daily with the word of God because then we see the transformation of things happening in our environments, our families, or our bodies. We can't afford not to renew our minds daily.

#renewyourmind

Day 16

Do not make friends with a hot-tempered person, do not associate with one easily angered, or you may learn their ways and get yourself ensnared.

Proverbs 22: 24-25 NIV

We all know a good friend can be hard to find. Let's be honest, friendships take work, like all relationships. This scripture reminds us of how much influence our friendships have in our lives. The question is, are you the influencer or being influenced? How important is it to you that your friendships draw you to God?

#**friendships**

Day 17

"Write the vision; make it plain on tablets, so he may run who reads it."

Habakkuk 2:2 ESV

A vision should always be written not just kept as an idea. I learned this over 15 years ago. I'll never forget the first time I heard this concept. It was youth Sunday. The speaker that day was a college student. She shared & showed us her "life vision." She had a nice three-ring binder with the vision she had for her life printed on paper. She identified each area of her life, and the vision for finances, her future spouse, and her career. I was told that we accomplish 80% of what we write down. What do you want to accomplish that you haven't, because you haven't written it down? Something shifts in the atmosphere when you write things down. The first step towards accountability is initiated once we write down our goals and visions. But remember only what we do for Christ will last.

#**visions**

Day 18

Take delight in the Lord, and he will give you the desires of your heart.

Psalm 37:4 NIV

God's word says He will give the desires of your heart when you take delight in Him. What are the true desires of your heart? Do your desires make your corner of the world a better place? Or are all your desires self-centered? Do these desires bring you closer to God? Do your desires fulfill God's purpose for your life?

#desires

Day 19

Those who are kind benefit themselves, but the cruel bring ruin on themselves.

Proverbs 11:17 NIV

Being kind to others doesn't cost us anything. Kindness is defined as the quality of being friendly, generous, and considerate. Sometimes I like to define words as I read God's word and then replace the word with the definition to make the bible more practical in my life. So, those who are friendly benefit themselves. Those who are generous benefit themselves. Those who are considerate benefit themselves. I don't know about you but I'd rather bring benefit than ruin to myself.

#bekind

Day 20

And without faith it is impossible to please God because anyone who comes to him must believe that he exists and that he rewards those who earnestly seek him.

Hebrews 11:6

When a person has faith, they operate in complete trust or confidence in someone or something. What or who do you place your trust in? Is your faith in your job, your spouse, or yourself? We should only place full faith in the Lord. After all He is not like man, He never disappoints or leads us astray.

#faith

Day 21

If you declare with your mouth, "Jesus is Lord," and believe in your heart that God raised him from the dead, you will be saved.

Romans 10:9 NIV

I come from a pentecostal background. I can remember as a child, at the end of service the pastor would always ask *"Are you saved, if you were to die today, would you be saved?"* That question always made me reflect "Am I saved" as if I had not declared and still believed. I think as humans, in our sinful nature, it's challenging to comprehend that I'm only required to do 2 things to be saved. Yes! Just 2 things. Please remember that. So, if you're reading this devotional today, and you're questioning "Am I saved" read Romans 10:9 again, do as it in-

structs, and let the matter be settled my brother
& sister because you ARE saved per God's word.

#saved

Day 22

Loyalty

Oneness

Virtuous

Endearment

These are just a few words that some may say to describe love. Love is an action not merely a word or feeling. If I say "I love you" but never show it through patience, kindness, gentleness, or selflessness, would you really think I love you? What's your definition of love? How do you practice your love walk? Do you act in love like the word of God instructs in 1 Corinthians 16:14. Or do you have to be in a relationship with someone to love them?

#**love**

Day 23

No weapon forged against you will prevail, and you will refute every tongue that accuses you.

Isaiah 54:17 NIV

Life always seems to offer warfare in some shape or form. For example financial issues, relations issues, or health issues. I proclaim today that no matter what you are facing, you have the VICTORY! No weapon formed against you shall prosper. Proclaim it with me. Say it aloud "NO WEAPEN FORMED AGAINST ME SHALL PROSPER." Now walk into the new atmosphere you just spoke into existence.

#noweapon

Day 24

Who is it that overcomes the world? Only the one who believes that Jesus is the Son of God.

1 John 5:5 NIV

Many times we wait to share how we've overcome trials & tribulations, but I am here to encourage you to share while you are still going through whatever situation you're facing. The word of God assures us that we are overcomers of the world once we've been born again. You already have the victory, my brother and sister. Today start operating from a place of victory not defeat. You are an overcomer. Your battle is already won.

#**overcomer**

Day 25

Do you not know that your body is a temple of the Holy Spirit, who is in you, whom you have received from God? You are not your own.

1 Corinthians 6:19 NIV

We know this scripture all too well. Often we use this scripture as motivation for eating healthy, exercising & sustaining from harmful substances to our bodies. Since our bodies are temples for the Holy Spirit we should be mindful to be respectful of it & replenish it. We show respect and replenish our bodies by spending time with God in His word. Let's be intentional by setting aside prayer time. We must also be mindful by guarding our spiritual entry gateways which are our minds, eyes & ears.

#temple

Day 26

Come and hear, all you who fear God; let me tell you what he has done for me.

Psalm 66:16

How often do you share your testimony? Testifying doesn't have to be this deep long-lasting experience that caused you tears, distress, & destitution. We can offer up a testimony of how good God has been to us. Yes! Simply sharing your gratitude for God waking you up this morning is a testimony. Take it even further, let your life be a daily testimony for God's glory.

#testify

Day 27

"For I know the plans I have for you," declares the Lord, "plans to prosper you and not to harm you, plans to give you hope and a future."

Jeremiah 29:11 NIV

Everyone seems to be on a quest to find purpose. Do you know the plans God has for you? Sometimes God will give us small insights into His plans for us through dreams, prophecies, or revelation through God's word. Just remember only what you do unto God will last. His purpose for your life will bring you all the things your heart longs for. After all, it will be what you were specifically designed to do.

#**purpose**

Day 28

Whatever you do, work at it with all your heart, as working for the Lord, not for human masters.

Colossians 3:23

I've been a physical therapist for 7 years. When I first started my journey I was super excited and passionate about the profession. As time passed my passions shifted. I credit my growth in Christ to the shift. However, in this current season, God still has me in the profession of PT. So, though it is no longer my passion, I'm still required to show up for my shift and deliver services to my patients as working for the Lord. This scripture helps me adjust my focus and steer from complaining because I'm not doing what I love. Patients often ask me "do you love what you do" I often reply, "why do you ask." Their reply is that "you seem so happy." Because I desire to please God, my desire manifests in my work.

#workingforGod

Day 29

For God created mankind in his own image, in the image of God he created them; male and female he created them.

Genesis 1:27 NIV

This scripture simply amazes me. When you ponder on being made in the image of our God, how does that make you feel? It makes me want to fully embrace who I am. It makes me feel that all my imperfections are perfectly imperfect. God made no mistakes when He created you. Start believing that!

You've heard it before, but let me remind you, there's only ONE of you. Can't nobody do you better than you. Believe that! Stop allowing people or yourself to convince you otherwise.

#embraceyou

Day 30

But if we hope for what we do not yet have, we wait for it patiently.

Romans 8:25 NIV

Life at some point or another will teach you a lesson of tolerance better known as patience. During the season of developing patience, your character is often molded. Mastering patience often means you don't get that job offer right away, but you're content not angry. Patience looks like waiting to meet your spouse while all your friends are getting married and starting families. Patience is being satisfied with your tiny apartment because the housing market isn't favorable for buyers in this season. My hope for you is that today, you embrace the capacity to tolerate any delay in your life without getting upset, angry, or coveting. What God has for you it is for you, my brother and sister.

#bepatient

Day 31

Being confident of this, that he who began a good work in you will carry it on to completion until the day of Christ Jesus.

Philippians 1:6

Each day that God awakes you, remember you've been given another opportunity to do something great, to make a positive impact on someone else's life, to simply be the YOU God is calling you to be. He has specific work, an assignment for you to complete. If only you are willing, God will be faithful and bring to completeness the work He called you to perform. Be you, not like your neighbor. There's someone waiting for you to do the work God gave you so they can begin theirs.

#**beyou**

Conclusion

I pray that as you close this devotional you've been encouraged, challenged, changed, & ready to #liveyourbestlife for Christ. Please remember that life & death are in the power of your tongue. Now go walk in your purpose.

With Love,
Vikkie J

www.ingramcontent.com/pod-product-compliance
Lightning Source LLC
Chambersburg PA
CBHW070759050426
42452CB00012B/2409